Searchlight
BOOKS™

Do You
Know the
Continents?

Learning
about
Africa

Robin Koontz

Lerner Publications • Minneapolis

Content Consultant: Raymond S. Mosha, Professor of Philosophy and Ethics, the Nelson Mandela University of Science and Technology, Arusha, Tanzania

Lerner Publications Company
A division of Lerner Publishing Group, Inc.
241 First Avenue North
Minneapolis, MN 55401 USA

For reading levels and more information, look up this title at www.lernerbooks.com.

Library of Congress Cataloging-in-Publication Data

Koontz, Robin Michal, author.
    Learning about Africa / by Robin Koontz.
        pages cm. — (Searchlight books. Do you know the continents?)
    Includes index.
    ISBN 978-1-4677-8013-1 (lb : alk. paper) — ISBN 978-1-4677-8343-9 (pb : alk. paper) — ISBN 978-1-4677-8344-6 (eb pdf)
    1. Africa—Geography—Juvenile literature. I. Title. II. Series: Searchlight books. Do you know the continents?
    DT12.25.K66 2015
    960—dc23   2015001952

1 – VP – 7/15/15

Contents

Chapter 1

LAND OF VARIETY

Where can you find great modern cities and rural villages? Where are the longest river and the biggest desert? Where do people speak more than one thousand different languages? The answer to all these questions is Africa.

Africa is a continent of many diverse cultures. How many languages are spoken there?

Land and Sea

Africa is approximately three times the size of the United States. It is the second-largest continent. Only Asia is larger.

Africa's Sahara Desert alone is about the same size as the United States.

Oceans and seas surround most of Africa. The Mediterranean Sea separates it from Europe to the north. The Atlantic Ocean lies to the west. The Indian Ocean lies to the east. Africa has just one land border with another continent. Its northeast area touches Asia.

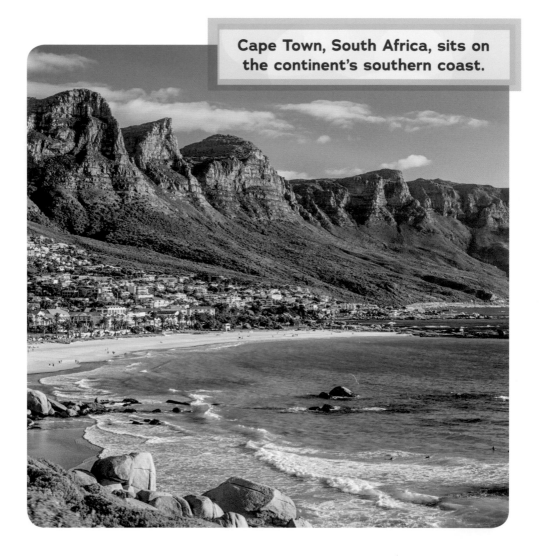

Cape Town, South Africa, sits on the continent's southern coast.

AFRICA COVERS ABOUT 11.7 MILLION SQUARE MILES (30.3 MILLION SQUARE KILOMETERS).

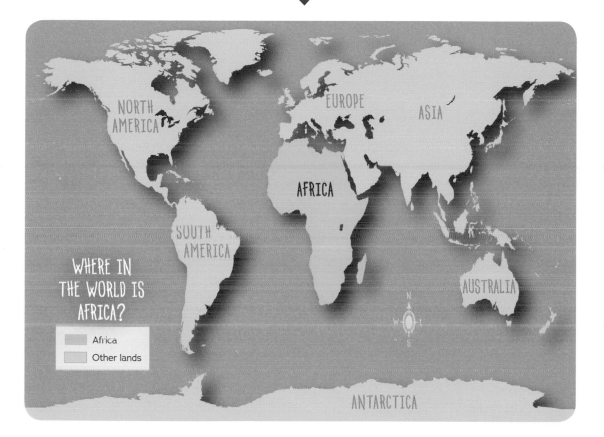

WHERE IN THE WORLD IS AFRICA?

Africa

Other lands

NORTH AMERICA

EUROPE

ASIA

AFRICA

SOUTH AMERICA

AUSTRALIA

ANTARCTICA

Modern Africa

Africa was once a place of small villages. But modern Africa is very different. The continent has a large number of huge cities. Lagos, Nigeria, for example, has more people than New York City.

Lagos is one of the fastest-growing cities in Africa.

Africa's national parks let visitors see amazing animals up close.

Many of Africa's animals roam in national parks. African governments set aside these areas to protect wildlife. Whether you want to explore a rain forest or a bustling city, Africa is an exciting place to visit!

Chapter 2

COUNTRIES AND CITIES

Scientists have found evidence that the first humans lived in East Africa. They evolved there about 250,000 years ago. Small tribes of people hunted animals. They gathered wild plants. Over thousands of years, people spread through Africa. They started communities and kingdoms all across the continent.

Scientists have found statues and other objects from ancient African kingdoms. Where do scientists think the first humans lived?

European Control

In the 1500s, European countries began taking many African people as slaves. Families were separated, and many people were killed. This continued for hundreds of years. By the late 1800s, most nations banned slavery.

Still, European countries continued taking advantage of Africa and its people. They wanted resources that were plentiful in the continent, such as gold and spices. They took land by force. The Europeans divided the continent between them. They set up colonies throughout Africa.

Europeans used modern weapons to control African colonies.

The African people wanted freedom. They wanted to control their own lands. After World War II (1939–1945), many European countries removed their colonies. A total of forty-seven African countries became independent between 1950 and 1980.

Nations, Cities, and Villages

By 2015, Africa had fifty-four countries. That's more than any other continent. The largest is Algeria. About 90 percent of Algeria is desert. Few people live in Africa's desert areas. The lands near Africa's rivers have many more people.

Tanganyika celebrated independence in 1961. It later became part of Tanzania.

HOW MANY AFRICAN COUNTRIES DO NOT TOUCH AN OCEAN? ARE ANY OF THEM CONTAINED WITHIN ANOTHER COUNTRY?

▼

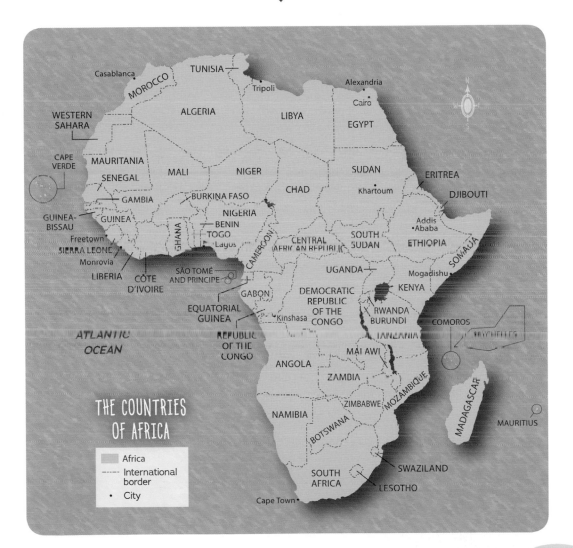

THE COUNTRIES OF AFRICA

- Africa
- - - - International border
- • City

The capital of Kenya is Nairobi.

Other countries include Ethiopia and Kenya in the east. Many countries sit on the western coast. They include Liberia, Guinea, and Ghana. The island nation of Madagascar lies southeast of the mainland.

Many cities, such as Mombasa, Kenya, and Johannesburg, South Africa, have more than one million people. More Africans are living in cities than ever before. In 1950, only about 15 percent lived in cities. That number has risen to 40 percent. The other 60 percent of people live in rural villages and on farms.

South Sudan

One of the world's newest countries is in Africa. South Sudan became independent in 2011. It split from Sudan. Its capital, Juba, sits on the Nile River. In 2013, a civil war broke out in the new country. Different groups tried to control the government. Peace agreements were signed in early 2015.

Chapter 3

LANDFORMS AND CLIMATE

Africa has a wide variety of landscapes and climates. Hot, dry deserts cover the north. Damp rain forests are found near the equator. Cool mountains and hills rise in the east.

Africa's landscapes feature a wide range of elevations. Where in Africa can you find mountains and hills?

Plains

Plains stretch through central Africa. They are called savannas. Grasses and other plants grow on these plains. One of these plants is called elephant grass. It can grow up to 10 feet (3 meters) tall! The savannas are mostly sunny. Farmers raise animals and grow crops there.

Grasses cover Africa's plains.

Deserts

The Sahara Desert in northern Africa is one of the world's largest deserts. But about 10,000 years ago, it was much rainier. The water made it possible for people to live there. By about 5,000 years ago, the rains slowed. The land became dry and sandy.

Modern people who live in the Sahara live near oases. These are places in deserts where there are pools of water. Plants can grow in these spots.

AFRICA'S RAIN FORESTS OFTEN HAVE RIVERS FLOWING THROUGH THEM.

▼

Africa's Forests

Africa's tropical rain forests are mostly near the equator. Up to 130 inches (330 centimeters) of rain falls per year in these places. The temperature stays warm all year.

Rain forests aren't Africa's only forests. Tropical woodlands border the rain forests. Their trees are spaced more widely than those in rain forests. Other forests exist in the highlands of eastern Africa. These places stay cooler due to their high altitudes.

Forests stretch along Africa's east coast.

**Lake Victoria was named after Queen
Victoria of the United Kingdom.**

African Waters

The Nile River is the world's longest river. It begins in
east-central Africa. The river flows north through Egypt.
It empties into the Mediterranean Sea. Africa also has
many big, deep lakes. Lake Victoria touches Kenya,
Uganda, and Tanzania. It is the second-largest lake on
Earth. Only Lake Superior in North America is bigger.

Mount Kilimanjaro is surrounded by flat plains.

Mountains and Highlands

Much of Africa is flat. But it does have high places. The Atlas Mountains run along the Mediterranean coastline. The Ethiopian Highlands lie in the east.

Africa's tallest peak is Mount Kilimanjaro. It is located in Tanzania. The mountain is a volcano. But it has not erupted in more than 100,000 years. Scientists think it may one day erupt again.

WHAT IS THE LARGEST CLIMATE ZONE IN THE NORTHERN PART OF AFRICA?

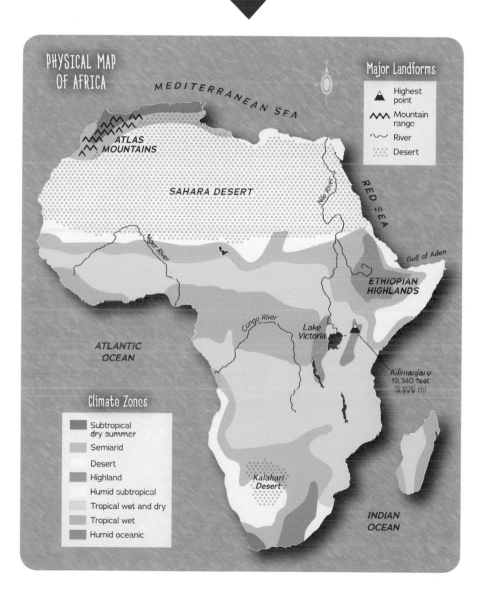

PHYSICAL MAP OF AFRICA

MEDITERRANEAN SEA

Major Landforms

- ▲ Highest point
- ᨈᨈ Mountain range
- ∿ River
- ⣿ Desert

ATLAS MOUNTAINS

SAHARA DESERT

Nile River

RED SEA

Niger River

Gulf of Aden

ETHIOPIAN HIGHLANDS

Congo River

Lake Victoria

ATLANTIC OCEAN

Kilimanjaro 19,340 feet (5,895 m)

Climate Zones

- Subtropical dry summer
- Semiarid
- Desert
- Highland
- Humid subtropical
- Tropical wet and dry
- Tropical wet
- Humid oceanic

Kalahari Desert

INDIAN OCEAN

Chapter 4

NATURAL RESOURCES

Africa is famous for its wildlife. Plants and animals are adapted to its diverse habitats. Some live in the hot deserts. Others survive on wide-open plains or in dense jungles.

Lions roam on Africa's savannas. What other habitats are in Africa?

On the Savanna

Many of Africa's most famous animals live on savannas. Giraffes and zebras graze there. Lions and cheetahs hunt them.

Baobab trees also live on savannas. These tall trees have very thick trunks. Many animals rely on these trees. Insects dig into them. Birds build nests in their branches. Baboons eat the trees' fruit.

Baobab trees store water in their huge trunks.

Rain Forests

African rain forests are home to thousands of different animals. Colorful birds fly above the trees. Countless insects buzz through the air. Monkeys and chimpanzees climb the trees. Gorillas walk the forest floor. Crocodiles and hippos lurk in rivers.

Fishing

Fishing provides Africa's people with food and money. Sardines and other small fish are found off the coast. Lakes and rivers are filled with freshwater fish. Lake Victoria is a key fishing area.

Some Africans make their living from the continent's rivers, lakes, and seas.

Endangered Animals

Many African animals are endangered. Hunting and habitat loss has put them at risk. Poachers capture or kill animals to sell their body parts. Laws guard these animals in many countries. African governments are working to protect them. They have created national parks and nature preserves. These areas give animals a safer place to live.

Chapter 5

PEOPLE AND CULTURES

The African continent contains a huge variety of peoples and cultures. Most Africans come from indigenous groups. They are descended from the original peoples of Africa. Other Africans are descended from immigrants. Immigrants came to Africa from Europe, Asia, and the Middle East.

Many of Africa's people combine traditional and modern cultures. From what cultural groups do most Africans descend?

Daily Life

Life in large African cities is similar to life in cities around the world. Wealthy Africans live similarly to people in American cities. People work in modern skyscrapers. They shop at supermarkets. They go to the movies. Nigeria has a huge movie industry.

However, life is very different for poor people in Africa's cities. They often have no electricity or running water. Some families live in a single small room.

Africa's large cities, such as Cairo, Egypt, look like cities in the United States.

Traditions

Some Africans follow old traditions. They live similarly to their ancestors. The Maasai people are famous for keeping their culture and language. They live in Tanzania and Kenya. Traditional clothing, music, and dances are part of many Maasai people's lives.

Religion

Christianity is common in central and southern Africa. Islam is common in north and east Africa. Africans all across the continent follow indigenous religions. Some Africans mix indigenous beliefs with newer religions.

The Maasai people hunt and farm to get their food.

The Pyramids of Giza

The Pyramids of Giza are some of the greatest human-made marvels in the world. The three pyramids stand on the banks of the Nile River near Cairo. The pyramids were completed in about 2500 BCE. They were tombs for ancient Egyptian kings. Khufu is the largest of the pyramids. It stands approximately 450 feet (137 m) high. It is made of more than two million stone blocks.

Chapter 6

ECONOMICS

Africa's economies are powered by farming, mining, tourism, and other industries. Modern African nations make money to build great cities. They make products that improve the lives of African people.

Africa's huge mines are filled with many useful minerals. What is another important industry for the continent?

Mining

Metals and minerals are found throughout Africa. Salt is harvested from the Sahara Desert. South African miners dig for gold. And Botswana is one of the biggest diamond producers on the planet.

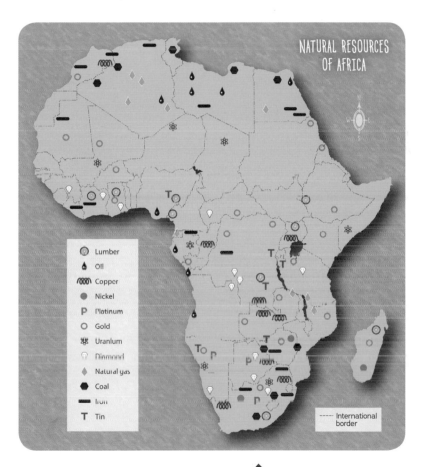

NATURAL RESOURCES OF AFRICA

Lumber	
Oil	
Copper	
Nickel	
P	Platinum
Gold	
Uranium	
Diamond	
Natural gas	
Coal	
Iron	
T	Tin

----- International border

WHAT KINDS OF RESOURCES ARE MOST COMMON IN SOUTHERN AFRICA?

Many tourists visit Africa to photograph animals.

Tourism

Africa's landscapes, coastlines, and wildlife make it popular with tourists. The continent has many hotels and restaurants. Tours called safaris let visitors see wild animals in national parks up close. Impressive historical sites, such as Egypt's pyramids, also draw tourists.

Poverty and Growth

Africa is rich in resources, but some of its people are very poor. Many of the continent's poorest people live in tiny, run-down homes. The new generation of Africans is working to change this. They are building up their continent and improving the lives of their people. There are many challenges. Poverty and violence are serious problems. But many of Africa's young people see a bright future for their continent.

Amazing Africa

Africa is an amazing continent. It has massive cities, huge deserts, and diverse cultures. Its rain forests and savannas hold an incredible mix of plants and wildlife. Where will your African adventure begin?

The African continent is full of stunning landscapes.

Exploring Africa

THE COUNTRIES OF AFRICA

Africa
International border
• City

Choose two or three countries or cities from the map above that you want to know more about. Choose places from different parts of Africa. Research these places online. What unique things are there to see and do? What do people eat? What local celebrations or festivals take place there? Write a paragraph about a trip that you will take to each place. What will you see and do?

Glossary

endangered: at risk of no longer existing. Overhunting and habitat destruction can lead to animals becoming endangered.

equator: the imaginary line that goes around the center of Earth

immigrant: a person who travels from one country to live in another

indigenous: people who originally lived in a place

mainland: the largest part of a country or continent

poverty: the state of being poor

rural: away from large cities

safari: a trip where people can see wild animals up close

savanna: a large area that is flat, covered in grass, and has few trees

tomb: a place where a person is buried

LERNER

SOURCE

Expand learning beyond the printed book. Download free, complementary educational resources for this book from our website, www.lerneresource.com.

Learn More about Africa

Books

Friedman, Mel. *Africa*. New York: Children's Press, 2009. Learn more about the people, landscapes, and animals of Africa.

Montgomery, Sy. *Chasing Cheetahs: The Race to Save Africa's Fastest Cats*. New York: Houghton Mifflin Harcourt, 2014. Read about the efforts in Africa to save endangered cheetahs.

Wojahn, Rebecca Hogue, and Donald Wojahn. *A Cloud Forest Food Chain: A Who-Eats-What Adventure in Africa*. Minneapolis: Lerner Publications, 2010. See how the plants and animals of Africa's forests depend on each other to survive.

Websites

Africa Map
http://worldmap.harvard.edu/africamap
Discover more about Africa using this interactive map. Learn about population, languages, conflicts, and more.

African Wildlife Foundation
http://www.awf.org
The African Wildlife Foundation works to ensure the wildlife and wild lands of Africa will endure forever.

Our Africa
http://www.our-africa.org
This website has videos made by African children from across the continent. They talk about their countries and their daily lives.

Index

Photo Acknowledgments

The images in this book are used with the permission of: © Pecold/Shutterstock Images, p. 4;
© GP232/iStockphoto, p. 5; © Dereje/Shutterstock Images, p. 6; © Laura Westlund/Independent
Picture Service, pp. 7, 13, 23, 33, 37; © Bill Kret/Shutterstock Images, p. 8; © W. L. Davies/
iStockphoto, p. 9; © Heritage Images/Corbis, p. 10; © duncan1890/iStockphoto, p. 11; © Bettmann/
Corbis, p. 12; © Syldavia/iStockphoto, p. 14; © Phototreat/iStockphoto, p. 15; © Dhoxax/iStockphoto,
p. 16; © Galyna Andrushko/Shutterstock Images, p. 17; © mariobono/iStockphoto, p. 18; © Pozzo Di
Borgo Thomas/Shutterstock Images, p. 19; © EcoPrint/Shutterstock Images, p. 20; © shujaa 777/
iStockphoto, p. 21; © graemes/iStockphoto, p. 22; © Maggy Meyer/Shutterstock Images,
p. 24; © guenterguni/iStockphoto, p. 25; © Andrea Willmore/Shutterstock Images, p. 26;
© Wolfgang Kaehler/Corbis, p. 27; © Pierre-Yves Babelon/Shutterstock Images, p. 28; © abalcazar/
iStockphoto, p. 29; © Kanokratnok/Shutterstock Images, p. 30; © Steven Allan/iStockphoto, pp. 31,
35; © Mark Schwettmann/Shutterstock Images, p. 32; © Nicola Margaret/iStockphoto, p. 34;
© JaySi/Shutterstock Images, p. 36.

Cover Image: © Planet Observer/Universal Images Group via Getty Images.

Main body text set in Adrianna Regular 14/20.
Typeface provided by Chank.